"If you desire a thriving faith in your marriage and family, *don't miss this book!*"

—BRUCE WILKINSON
author of the #1 *New York Times* bestseller *The Prayer of Jabez*

"I'm delighted to endorse *Growing a Spiritually Strong Family*. As the Raineys say, 'It's not words by themselves that communicate love—it's talking with your children in a way that shows deep interest and a strong desire to be involved in their lives.'"

—ELISABETH ELLIOT

"More than ever before, we need strong and loving families. I so appreciate how Dennis and Barbara continually emphasize the importance of centering our families upon a relationship with Christ."

—GARY SMALLEY

"The Raineys have outlined ten 'spiritual seeds' that are designed to help you create the ideal environment for growing the strong family that God intended."

—DR. TONY EVANS
pastor of Oak Cliff Bible Fellowship and president of *The Urban Alternative*

"Championship teams in sports are not made overnight. It takes time, energy, sacrifice, and a solid game plan. If what you desire is a *championship* family, please allow Dennis and Barbara Rainey the opportunity to help coach you with a winning game plan in *Growing a Spiritually Strong Family*."

—JOSE ALVAREZ
husband, dad, and former major league pitcher with the Atlanta Braves

F a m i l y  *F i r s t*

GROWING A
SPIRITUALLY
Strong
FAMILY

DENNIS & BARBARA
RAINEY

with BRUCE NYGREN

Multnomah® Publishers *Sisters, Oregon*

GROWING A SPIRITUALLY STRONG FAMILY
published by Multnomah Publishers, Inc.
© 2002 by Dennis and Barbara Rainey
International Standard Book Number: 1-57673-778-0

Cover design by Christopher Gilbert/UDG DesignWorks
Cover image by Zefa Germany/Index Stock Photography

Scripture quotations are from:
New American Standard Bible
© 1960, 1977 by the Lockman Foundation

Multnomah is a trademark of Multnomah Publishers, Inc.,
and is registered in the U.S. Patent and Trademark Office.
The colophon is a trademark of Multnomah Publishers, Inc.

Printed in the United States of America

For information:
MULTNOMAH PUBLISHERS, INC.
POST OFFICE BOX 1720
SISTERS, OREGON 97759

Library of Congres Cataloging-in-Publication Data

Rainey, Dennis, 1948-
   Growing a spiritually strong family / by Dennis and Barbara Rainey with Bruce Nygren.
      p. cm.
Includes bibliographical references.
   ISBN 1-57673-778-0 (hardback)
   1. Family--religious life. 2. Family--Religious aspects--Christianity. I. Rainey,
Barbara. II. Nygren, Bruce. III. Title.
   BV4526.2 .R34 2002
   248.8'45--dc21

02 03 04 05 06 07 08—10 9 8 7 6 5 4 3 2 1 0

TABLE OF CONTENTS

Acknowledgments

E very book, large or small, inevitably involves a cast of individuals who play key roles along the way. The following people deserve a standing ovation for their work on this book.

First and foremost we want to express our deep appreciation to Bruce Nygren. As you know, Bruce, this book was shaped during some very difficult days for you and your family. Thank you for your friendship and your love for Jesus Christ, His Word, and the institution of the family.

We also want to thank:

The support team in the executive director's office at FamilyLife: Janet Logan, John Majors, and Cherry Tolleson. You are there day after day backing us up.

Members of other departments at FamilyLife who assisted: Ben Colter, Merle Engel, Clark Hollingsworth, Bob Lepine, Doug Martin, Tammy Meyers, Tonda Nations, and Bob Paine. And a special word of appreciation to a servant no longer on active duty but still on call: Pat Claxton.

Our colaborers at Multnomah Publishers: Don Jacobson, Bill Jensen, David Kopp, Cliff Boersma, and David Webb. A special word of thanks for an editing job well done goes to Jim Lund.

The Promise Keepers organization, for giving Dennis the awesome opportunity to speak to thousands of men on the topic "25 Ways to Spiritually Lead Your Wife." That message sparked the idea for this book.

THIS BOOK IS DEDICATED TO OUR
SIX MARRIED CHILDREN:

Ashley and Michael Escue

Ben and Marsha Kay Rainey

Samuel and Stephanie Rainey

IT IS OUR PRAYER THAT YOUR
MARRIAGES AND FAMILIES WILL
GROW EVER STRONGER IN CHRIST!

—*Dennis and Barbara Rainey*—

INTRODUCTION

After all these years, the Rainey family still remembers the night I (Dennis) came home from work and found the dishwasher inoperative, the garbage disposal stopped up, and the house looking like the aftermath of a simultaneous flood and tornado. Our three-year-old was sick, crushed cereal nuggets littered the floor, and our twelve-month-old reached for a hug from her daddy with hands dripping melted chocolate chips. Our five-year-old waved a cast, her broken arm still mending, and our ten- and eight-year-olds complained in duet of stomach upsets.

My wife, Barbara, looked ready to run for the hills. If she'd left, I probably would have been right behind her.

If you have children yourself, you know what we mean. The problem with a family is that it is so *daily!*

There are good times and times not so good. Being married and raising a family are not for the faint of heart. The journey is long and demanding. Yet we parents know that what we are doing day after day has meaning far beyond these few years we have with our children.

A recent FamilyLife survey among American churchgoers asked the question, "Which issues do you currently need help with in your life?"[1] Of the answers given most frequently, three of the top four concerns related to spiritual disciplines and growth. As a nation, we are desperately seeking a deeper spiritual life for our children and ourselves. Yet we live in a culture that discourages spiritual growth at every turn.

Do these issues resonate with you, too? Then this little book is for you. We believe it offers the immediate encouragement and direction your family needs. It's an invitation to push aside the distractions that surround you and refocus on what really counts: God, His Word, family, and eternity.

After nearly thirty years of marriage (make that sixty years—there are two of us!), leading a national ministry, and parenting six children, we have identified ten critical factors in raising a spiritually strong family. If you and your family apply these sound biblical principles and practices, we guarantee that you'll discover a growing spiritual vitality in your home. We can promise this boldly because it is not just our desire for our families and ourselves—it is God's desire as well.

This book also includes ten "spiritual seeds"—practical, uplifting activities for you and your mate that will nurture your family's faith. If you don't have a mate, keep reading—we've written this text primarily for couples, but the principles apply just as much to the single mom or dad.

No matter where you are in your journey as a parent, be encouraged that God is with you and that He values your role as spiritual leader of your family. It is an effort worth the long days—and the sometimes longer nights:

Therefore, my beloved brethren, be steadfast, immovable, always abounding in the work of the Lord, knowing that your toil is not in vain in the Lord. (I Corinthians 15:58)

May God bless and keep you as you grow a spiritually strong family.

Dennis and Barbara Rainey

1

SINK YOUR ROOTS

It arrived without warning. I (Dennis) was at work when I happened to look out the window; the beautiful blue sky I'd admired minutes earlier was now filled with ominous black clouds. Soon rain pelted the ground, followed by a fierce wind that twisted trees at an impossible angle. Then the tornado siren shrieked. We scrambled away from our desks and searched for cover; many of us huddled under a concrete stairwell in the basement. The radio confirmed our greatest fear—the tornado was headed our way.

As 120-mph winds shattered windows and shook the walls, several of us prayed. I thought of my family and prayed for their safety (I discovered later that the tornado missed our home by less than three blocks). After five harrowing minutes, the wind subsided and the sun returned. We'd survived! Thankfully, no one was hurt.

I stepped outside to view the damage. The tornado had touched down just fifty feet away, tearing out several massive pine trees before hopping over our office building and uprooting more monster pines. I was surprised to see that the root clumps of the uprooted trees were not that large. Then I noticed, not far away, a majestic, ancient oak that looked almost untouched. It was missing just a few broken limbs.

Later I learned that the pine trees in our region have a shallow root system, which is why several of those green, towering beauties became firewood. But the root system of an oak tree plunges deep into the soil, enabling it to withstand even a tornado's fury.

The roots make the difference.

What kind of spiritual root system does a healthy Christian family require? If we want to develop unshakable leadership for a family—the kind of strength that will resist life's tornadoes—we need spiritual roots like the oak tree. The best way we know to ensure such deep roots is to first make sure the parents are becoming "oaks of righteousness" (Isaiah 61:3). Parents need to grow in their faith and become sturdy disciples of Christ. Jesus said:

> "Abide in Me, and I in you. As the branch cannot bear fruit of itself unless it abides in the vine, so neither can you unless you abide in Me. I am the

vine, you are the branches; he who abides in Me and I in him, he bears much fruit, for apart from Me you can do nothing." (John 15:4–5)

Followers of Christ have understood for centuries the critical importance of certain spiritual activities that mark the life of a growing disciple. We will list three basics, though certainly there are more. If you will make a priority of just these, you will develop a deep root system that will bear up against the storms of life and make you and your spouse steady spiritual leaders of your family.

A PERSONAL DAILY EXPERIENCE WITH JESUS CHRIST

To grow and become all that God created you to be, you must submit to Jesus Christ as lord, master, and maker of your life. The spiritual journey of following Him is not a list of do's and don'ts, but rather a moment-by-moment encounter with Jesus. Growth occurs in our lives as we submit to Him, walk with Him by faith, and obey Him.

The following is not a checklist, but rather proven spiritual disciplines that help us grow as followers of Him. How you go about implementing them is your call, but applying these basics over time will transform a "baby Christian" into a mature follower of Christ.

- *Prayer.* Good communication is the key in any thriving relationship. This is certainly true with

God, too. Scripture urges us to "pray without ceasing" (I Thessalonians 5:17), to pray about everything (Philippians 4:6–7), and in prayer to give thanks in everything (I Thessalonians 5:18).

• *Bible Study.* Scripture is our owner's manual for the Christian life. Make the Bible your constant go-to source for decision making, for the truth about God's character, His ways, and His promises, and for tips on how better to follow Him.

• *Worship.* We are commanded to worship God, individually and collectively. If we are failing to faithfully worship God, not just on Sunday but in our everyday moments, we probably are worshiping something else.

• *Giving/Service.* We are stewards of many personal, material, and financial resources. God has told us that it is better to give than to receive. We need to reap the joy of giving graciously like our Father in heaven gives to us. A type of giving is to serve others in the name of Christ, particularly those who are destitute or lonely.

• *Fellowship.* Don't miss out on a huge benefit of being a Christian—connection to the body of Christ. When you and your family assemble together (Hebrews 10:25) in a strong local church—a place where the Scriptures are taught as God's inspired

Word—the wisdom and encouragement of fellow believers will help you effectively lead and grow your family spiritually.

• *Witness.* We have the job of acting on Jesus' behalf to reconcile the lost to God. This includes befriending neighbors and others who are not believers and planting and reaping the seeds of the Gospel.

TRUE FRIENDS

Spiritual growth usually occurs in the context of relationships. We all need people close to us—not just to enjoy friendship and fellowship, but also to reap the benefits of mutual accountability. Both the husband and wife need at least one close, same-sex Christian friend (this is especially true for a single parent). And at least one other couple needs to know how the two of you are doing in your marriage.

We have a pair of friends, a couple, upon whom we frequently lean for counsel, advice, and balance. We discuss everything from discipling children to finances, home maintenance, managing pressure, and even thorny theological issues. We have experienced the "sheltering tree" of their friendship.

A small group of peers can often provide these accountability relationships. Ideally you will be part of a group of friends who are all seeking to grow individually and together as followers of Christ. (See page 96 for information about HomeBuilders, the world's fastest-growing small group study.)

AUTHENTIC LIVING

Real life begins at home. The toughest place to be a daily, consistent follower of Christ is around the house. When you are at home, surrounded by a mate who knows you well and several little disciples who are intently observing your every word and move, it's hard to keep up a front for long. And you shouldn't. If you have a vital relationship with Jesus Christ, just live it out as honestly and consistently as you can. God will take care of the rest.

There are many ways to show your family that you are serious about following in the footsteps of Jesus Christ, but two in particular really count: Admitting your mistakes and asking for forgiveness when you mess up in a relationship—especially with one of your children.

As humbling as it is, quite often you can get a "two

SPIRITUAL
SEED NO. 1

Within the next three weeks, invite a Christian couple that you enjoy and trust over for dinner. Ask if they will be your "marriage accountability partners" (and if they say yes, serve them both an extra scoop of ice cream!).

for one" and demonstrate both of these qualities at the same time! It's best to initiate this approach when your children are small. (Then it may not feel so humiliating when they're older!)

I (Barbara) remember a time when our daughter, Ashley, was about four months old. I was attempting to change her diaper, and she was being extra squirmy. I didn't explode and yell at her, but I was impatient. My conscience was tweaked. I thought, *I should apologize to her. But does this make sense? She's only a few months old! She won't remember or understand.* Yet I knew it was the chance to begin a pattern of apologizing when I made a mistake with my child. I told Ashley I was sorry and asked her to forgive me. That apology was good for her *and* me!

> *That apology was good for her* and *me!*

When this happens with an older child, I believe the key is to tell your daughter or son what Scripture says God expects from us when we wrong another person. If we brush things aside, in effect we are sending the message, "I did this and that's okay. But *you* can't get away with it." That's when children get very confused. But when a parent can admit a mistake to a child, ask for forgiveness, and take the whole situation to God, then there is hope you both will learn from your mistake. Spiritual growth can't occur in a heart that is too stubborn to admit its mistakes.

When our son, Samuel, was fifteen, I (Dennis) was supposed to pick him up after a tennis practice. I had told him I might be a few minutes late in order to wrap up tasks at the office. But an urgent phone call came in, and I ended up arriving fifty minutes late. Samuel was nowhere in sight. After many more minutes I finally caught up with him.

When Samuel climbed in the car, I looked him in the eye and said, "Son, I am really sorry. I let you down. I want you to be able to count on me as your dad. Will you forgive me?"

"Sure Dad, no problem," he said.

Does that sound simple? It is—sort of. Admitting your faults to your teenage son takes some courage and swallowing of pride. But if we want every member of the family to be spiritually strong, we have to respond to our Lord and walk the way He walked—not just talk about it.

How is your root system? Does it barely reach below the surface, or does it stretch deep into the soil? Invest the necessary time and energy to be "like a tree planted by the water, that extends its roots by a stream and will not fear when the heat comes; but its leaves will be green, and it will not be anxious in a year of drought nor cease to yield fruit" (Jeremiah 17:8).

Isn't that what we all seek? We want a family of fruitful "trees" that flourish no matter what—a grove filled with "oaks of righteousness."

2

PRAY WITH YOUR MATE

We've offered this advice to millions of couples. Nothing we've said has done more to change the course of their lives.

Pray with your mate.

Yet when I (Dennis) first heard this advice, I was underwhelmed.

At the time Barbara and I married (quite a while ago—sometime in the latter half of the twentieth century!) my boss was a mature, successful Christian leader named Carl Wilson. Since Carl had been married for more than twenty-five years and was obviously a happy husband and father, I thought I should tap into his wisdom on marriage. Not long after our honeymoon I asked him, "Carl, what is the very best piece of advice you could give me as we start our marriage together?"

Carl didn't even hesitate.

"Oh, that's easy, Denny," he said. "Pray every day with Barbara. I've prayed every day with my Sara Jo for more than twenty-five years. Nothing has built our marriage more than our prayer time together."

The answer seemed simplistic—the kind of response that makes you want to say, "That's nice, but is there something else?" Yet the years have shown that Carl's advice was profound and priceless.

We began praying together every day, usually at night before going to sleep. Except for times when travel separates us—and even then we pray together over the telephone—our guess is that we have missed this daily custom fewer than a dozen times in nearly thirty years of marriage.

That does not mean this spiritual discipline is always easy or pleasant. The enemy of our souls does everything he can to deter us from talking to God. And he seems especially intent on stopping a husband and wife from sharing in this powerful spiritual intimacy.

We both remember one night when, to say it delicately, we were not enjoying one another. Actually we were arguing about something. I climbed into bed and noticed that all I could see of the normally cordial Barbara was her back—as far to her edge of the mattress as she could go without falling to the floor. I had a similar outlook on our relationship and settled in on the extreme edge on my side. Between our two backs was an emotional Grand Canyon—filled with ice. The idea of praying together and then exchanging a goodnight kiss was less than appealing.

But before I could drop off to sleep, I felt as if someone had tapped me on the shoulder. It wasn't Barbara. Then a voice seemed to whisper, *Rainey, are you going to pray with her tonight?*

Don't you just hate it when God won't leave you alone when you want

Lord, back off! Don't confuse me with details and facts!

to indulge your self-pity and sin? I stalled for time. In my thoughts I replied, *No, Lord, I'm not going to pray with her tonight. I don't even like her tonight.*

His answer was swift: *Yes, I know. That is why you need to pray with her.*

But Lord, You know that this time she is 90 percent wrong!

And it's your 10 percent of fault that is causing her to be 90 percent wrong.

Lord, back off! And don't confuse me with details and facts!

I continued to debate with God, listing the reasons why my feelings were justifiably wounded and Barbara needed to repent—first. He didn't buy it. Finally He said, *Aren't you the one who tells the couples at your FamilyLife marriage conferences that you pray with Barbara every night?*

That's a cheap shot, Lord!

But after that I knew my self-righteous pout and plot were doomed. I finally rolled into that icy demilitarized zone in the center of the bed and whispered to Barbara, "Sweetheart, will you forgive me for being 10 percent wrong?"

No—I didn't say that! Even as a new husband I had learned a few things! I did gulp and stammer—some words are covered with Velcro and stick by your Adam's apple. I sure did not want to say, "I'm sorry." I still felt so right about my side in our argument. But I finally pried out the words that needed to be said: "Sweetheart, will you forgive me?" That led to a loving truce that allowed us to end our day praying together.

This daily practice helps us dissolve and resolve disagreements and keeps us closely connected—no small feat for any couple in today's stressful, fast-paced world!

WHY IS PRAYING TOGETHER A STRUGGLE?

You may agree that praying as a couple is essential in giving spiritual leadership to a family, but you also may be wondering why it can be so hard for a husband and wife to just take each other by the hand, bow heads, and seek God's guidance and help for a particular need. In

Isaiah 65:24 we read, "It will also come to pass that before they call, I will answer; and while they are still speaking, I will hear." It makes no sense that children of God should avoid such a potent source of wisdom and power—but couples do in huge numbers.

Surveys taken at FamilyLife Marriage Conferences show that less than 8 percent of all couples pray together regularly; we estimate that less than 3 percent of all Christian couples have *daily* prayer together.

God wants marriage to be a three-way, lifelong spiritual relationship between a man, a woman, and God. Since He's so intimately involved, wouldn't it be natural for God to desire that couples bring their needs and praises to Him on a daily basis?

We honestly can say that we do not know what might have happened to our marriage or even if we would still be together if we had not faithfully followed Carl's "simple" advice from our newlywed days.

Most important, this consistent practice has reinforced our commitment to keep Jesus Christ the Lord of the Rainey home. And why would we not want that? He's the One who said, "If two of you agree on earth about anything that they may ask, it shall be done for them by My Father who is in heaven. For where two or three have gathered together in My name, I am there in their midst" (Matthew 18:19–20).

Parents need that kind of clout! Over the years the two of us have asked God for just about everything—big deals, little deals, and every deal in between. For instance, when our boys were fourteen and twelve they began to maul each other like professional wrestlers. The roughhousing got so bad that one night they ripped a door off its hinges.

After we disciplined them and made them pay for the damage, we offered one of those prayers of desperate parents: "Lord, we feel like we are losing this battle with our boys. Will you find some way to knit their hearts together?"

The two of us have asked God for just about everything.

Several days later our oldest son, Benjamin, asked to talk with us. The previous night he had dreamed that his brother was killed in a car accident. Benjamin woke up crying because he missed Samuel. He felt convicted that he was not really appreciating his brother and wanted to become a better older brother.

Although this experience didn't end the sibling war, it tempered the battling. It was exciting for us to see God answer our prayer by divinely orchestrating that circumstance.

Getting Started

Sometimes the most difficult step is the first one. If praying together as a couple is a struggle, here are some ideas on how to overcome the inhibitions you may feel:

• *First, make a commitment to pray together daily.* In this, I (Dennis) urge husbands to take the lead. I have a stack of business cards with e-mail addresses from men who have committed to pray with their wives every day. Over the years I've heard story after story of men who fought through their fears and "stepped up" by leading their wives in prayer. As I write this I've just heard from a successful businessman who, after making this commitment just a month before, reports his marriage is already growing in intimacy and satisfaction. Even his children have seen the difference!

Make the commitment. Tell your spouse that "from now on, we will pray together every day." And send your e-mail address to me at www.familylife.com. I still write to men and ask them if they are praying with their wives.

• *Second, if you are wondering how to pray and what to pray about, use the ACTS method:*

A is for *ADORATION:* Worship and adore God for His love, grace, forgiveness, and work in your lives, marriage, and family.

C is for *CONFESSION:* Agree with God about sin that needs to be confessed before you make your petitions in prayer to God.

T is for *THANKSGIVING:* Thank God for your spouse, your children, your job, and your home. Thank God for His provision for your lives together.

S is for *SUPPLICATION:* Now ask God for help with those matters that are heavy on your heart: for example, a child that is struggling with you or at school, physical and spiritual needs in your family, and financial troubles. Go to God with your requests—He loves you and wants to hear your petitions. Also, keep in mind that God is not impressed with religious language. So keep your prayers to your heavenly Father reverent yet relational.

•*Third, take turns praying.* One person can pray one night and then the other can pray the next night. Or take turns

SPIRITUAL
SEED No. 2

Making prayer a habit just takes practice. So put down this book right now, find your mate (a phone call works just as well if you're far apart), and offer a short prayer to God. Just don't forget where you stopped reading!

praying each night as a couple. When we struggle with different issues in our roles as husband or wife, prayer becomes the place where these burdens are cast upon Him.

The point is *doing it!* If you haven't prayed together regularly, will you do your family a favor and start this great habit today?

3

GIVE YOUR CHILDREN YOU

Do you know what is likely *the* most valuable gift you can give your children? It's not your old pickup, a college education, or even your reputation for integrity. They'll benefit from all of those things—but your children ultimately want more than your stuff, your wealth, and your good family name. What they want and need *most* is a relationship with you. They want to know your heart. They want *you*. And if they don't get you, they are less likely to know and give themselves to God.

This truth about what children want applies to all ages. I (Dennis) remember my first "date" with Ashley when she was just three years old. I called her from the office and said, "Hi, Princess, this is Dad. I would really like to have a special date with you tonight."

She giggled. Then I heard her say to Barbara in an excited voice, "Daddy wants to take me out on a date!"

A short time later I pulled up in front of the house, walked to the front door and knocked. When Barbara opened it, I said, "Hello ma'am, is your daughter home?" Ashley pranced out in her finest dress. We held hands as we walked to our old station wagon. I opened her door and she scrambled in.

Right then

I turned into

a pool of

melted butter.

As we drove away she slipped her little arm around my neck. We went to a restaurant and ate chocolate pie and chocolate ice cream—washed down with chocolate milk. Then we drove to a theater where Ashley had a great time crawling over the seats and occasionally watching *Bambi.* We ate popcorn. We spilled popcorn. We drank soft drinks. We spilled soft drinks.

On the way home, the faint green light from the dashboard lighting our faces, I asked, "Ashley, what was your favorite thing about tonight?"

She patted me on the arm with her little hand and said, "Just being with you, Dad; just being with you." It's too bad we'd spilled all that popcorn, because right then I turned into a pool of melted butter.

To this day I still enjoy dating our teenage daughters. It's my chance to have fun with them, catch up on how they're doing, and stay connected.

A parent who lavishes love on a child through intense involvement mirrors what God does for all of His children: "I have loved you with an everlasting love; therefore I have drawn you with lovingkindness" (Jeremiah 31:3). When we give ourselves without reservation to our children, we draw them to us. A child who knows the love of a parent through a multitude of shared experiences receives a taste of the beautiful relationship God wants to have with each of His precious ones.

Children often see God when they look at their parents. Our influence in this role—and our responsibility—is great. When we model qualities of our Father in heaven by allowing the love of Jesus Christ to flow through us and into our children, we're succeeding as parents.

We do not propose a complicated, deeply theological set of practices to make this happen. Our advice is simple and summarized by three Ts: *time, touch,* and *talk.* These three Ts make a relationship with our child a reality. And through this relationship our child begins to grow the roots of a spiritual life.

TIME

We have yet to meet a child (or an adult, for that matter) who feels deeply loved when he is given only occasional bursts of "quality time." Children don't seem to understand this concept. When they want mom and dad, they want mom and dad.

Parenting children just takes time. How that time is disbursed varies as they grow older—and when your little guys and gals become teenagers, you may want them to give *you* some quality time! But their need for you to be available and flexible with your time never changes.

This creates a definite challenge in today's fast-paced culture, especially if you are a single parent. Since time is finite, we must set priorities for our schedule. We encourage you to carefully consider how you spend your time and whether or not you are available to your children.

My (Dennis's) schedule has always been demanding, but by the time we had graduated four children from high school, the responsibilities of a daily radio program, writing, speaking, and travel began to take me away from home even more frequently. It was Barbara's gentle and persistent admonishment that ultimately caused me to adjust my schedule and focus so that I could have a better relationship with our two teenage daughters still at home.

As a result, I am more involved in their lives and the

issues they face—dating, peer pressure, boundaries, and more. The bottom line: My teenage daughters need a dad who will love them *and* speak the truth to them. They know I care because I am there—*all* there!

SPIRITUAL
SEED No. 3

*Arrange your schedule
so that you can spend
an hour or more
of uninterrupted time
with each of your
children during the next
week. And when
you're together, take note
of the wonderful look
of joy you'll discover in
your child's face.*

TOUCH

You can also make your children feel loved by giving them plenty of physical touch. Regular hugs, kisses, and hand holding all say "you are loved."

When they are little, make sure your tykes have plenty of time in your lap to cuddle. And although you should be hugging your children for no reason at all, be sure to create special moments of affection each day—like bed-time kisses. We still kiss our children good night, even though they are teenagers and adults.

Your arrival at home after a day at work or an afternoon of running errands presents another great opportunity to offer affection. When our children were smaller, we turned these greeting times into "The Bear Hug Routine." I (Dennis) would get near Deborah, for instance, and say, "Do you want a baby bear hug, a mama bear hug, or a daddy bear hug?" The answer would be a giggle and "a baby bear." So I would give Deborah a light squeeze and say "eek, eek, eek"—the sound a baby bear might make.

Then Deborah would say in a little voice, "I want a mama bear hug, too, Daddy!"

So this time I would wrap my arms around her, squeeze harder, and say, "Mmmmmmmmmmmmmm."

As a parent

"Now I want a daddy bear hug!" Deborah would hold very still, arms straight at her sides, eyes shut tight. I would pick her up, squeeze like crazy, and yell, "Growwwwwwwwwwwwwl!" amidst shrieks of laughter. Even now, years later, Deborah laughs and smiles when I ask if she wants a bear hug.

you must never

back off from

giving this

affection.

As a parent you must never back off from giving this affection. When your sons and daughters are teenagers, it may feel awkward—but don't stop. They still need your loving touch.

I (Barbara) learned this one day from Benjamin, one of my teenage sons. My "baby" now towered above me; I had to reach up to plant a kiss on his cheek. The scratch of his emerging beard on my face reminded me that this almost-adult would soon be leaving home for good. I hugged him, let go, and tried to step back—and was pleasantly surprised when he held on tight. He seemed to be thinking, *Don't stop. I may look grown up, I may look like I don't need it, but please don't stop. I love this more than I can let on.* I didn't let go!

TALK

We often hear adults say things like, "I think I would have gotten along better with my mom and dad if we had just talked more."

Now is your chance to create a new model. A spiritually strong family is built on a foundation of "relational concrete." Tell your children your values, expectations, goals, and dreams for them, your family, and yourself. Ask them about their worries and their own dreams and goals. It's not words by themselves that communicate love—it's talking with your children in a way that shows deep interest and a strong desire to be involved in their lives.

Talking became even more important during the days following the terrorist attacks on the World Trade Center and the Pentagon. Laura, then sixteen, wanted to know if this was the beginning of the Tribulation. And Deborah, then eighteen, asked if World War III had begun. Both questions led to a healthy discussion about their fears and the future. We also took the opportunity to remind them about the character of God—His sovereign rule, mercy, love, and desire that we share the Gospel with others. All these discussions took place because we have a good relationship with our daughters.

This loving conversation begins while your baby is still in the womb. It grows and matures throughout a child's development; when your child reaches adulthood you can communicate like friendly peers.

Talking may be a challenge during the teenage years, but it's more important at this time than ever. Many teenagers—boys especially—just do not seem to want to talk. But don't give up. You must pursue them—a persistent, gentle priming of the conversation well. Be prepared for that moment when the mood shifts and the words literally gush out of your teenager's mouth. Give your teen your full attention; listen well before you respond.

Talking may be a challenge during the teenage years, but it's more important at this time than ever.

We'll never forget the struggle we had when one of our teenage sons didn't want to talk to us. It was a constant challenge to initiate a relationship because he felt he could do just fine without us. Over and over we reminded each other that we were the adults and the teenager was the child, and that what he needed from us was mature, adult love—not immature rejection.

It's easy in such situations to feel hurt and withdraw, but that is the opposite of what your teen needs. We loved our son and kept on pursuing a relationship. It wasn't easy, but it kept us connected and involved in his life. In the end our son benefited because he had two parents who never stopped loving and believing in him. We feel that our relationship with him may have kept him out of a lot of trouble.

Our model in being available and giving ourselves to our children is a good one. Jesus said, "Behold, I stand at the door and knock; if anyone hears My voice and opens the door, I will come in to him, and will dine with him, and he with Me" (Revelation 3:20). That picture of a loving God knocking and waiting, eager to enter a life, is how our children should perceive us. Just as He does for us, always strive to give your children *you.*

4

EAT RIGHT

Does your diet contain the right nutrients to keep you healthy?

Our government requires a listing of nutritional facts on food and beverage packages. Most of us are interested in total calories per serving—especially calories coming from "good" or "bad" fat. An athlete might be most interested in the carbohydrate count. A person battling a disease might evaluate the presence of certain vitamins or dietary fiber. Others are most concerned about cholesterol.

Perhaps our favorite nutritional fact list appears on bottled water—all zeroes, nothing! A dieter's dream!

While the nutritional fact list works well for food required by our physical body, what if a similar kind of list on other products evaluated spiritual content? What if every TV program, book, video, or music CD revealed its percentage of the "recommended daily allowance" of spiritual necessities like holiness, truth, forgiveness, character, perseverance, grace, justice, fruits of the spirit, repentance, and so on? How would each product (including this one) rate?

Unfortunately, the spiritual fact list for today's prime-time TV shows wouldn't even compare to bottled water. The label for most shows would reveal ingredients that are deeply harmful to spiritual values. Many other media productions would fare almost as poorly.

Fewer than four of ten born-again Christians read the Bible on their own in a typical week.

There is one "product," however, that is guaranteed to provide everyone in your family with the perfect blend of spiritual nourishment: the Bible.

It's a tragedy that although most Christians today express a deep fondness for Scripture, they are apparently failing to feast on the Word. Researcher George Barna reported early in 2001 that fewer than four of ten born-again Christians read the Bible on their own in a typical week.[2] There's a word for that—*starvation.* A FamilyLife survey conducted in churches throughout the United States shows that two-thirds of couples only occasionally—if at all—read or discuss the Bible together. Just 15 percent of couples discuss the Bible several times a week or more.[3]

If you want a spiritually healthy family, you must make sure that each member consumes a healthy diet of the everlasting Word of God.

How you decide to do this is up to you. We'll offer some of our own thoughts, but just as individual food tastes, dishes, and styles of cooking vary widely, so can methods of consuming Scripture. The manner of eating is not important; just be sure you eat your fill every day.

WHAT THE BIBLE SAYS ABOUT THE BIBLE

If you need any convincing on the importance of Scripture to your spiritual diet, consider this verse:

> "Ho! Every one who thirsts, come to the waters; and you who have no money come, buy and eat. Come, buy wine and milk without money and without cost. Why do you spend money for what is not bread, and your wages for what does not satisfy? Listen carefully to Me, and eat what is good, and delight yourself in abundance." (Isaiah 55:1–2)

The Psalms are full of statements urging us to consume God's "law"—His Word—for our own good:

> The law of the LORD is perfect, restoring the soul; the testimony of the LORD is sure, making wise the simple. The precepts of the LORD are right, rejoicing the heart; the commandment of the LORD is pure, enlightening the eyes. (Psalm 19:7–8)
>
> Then they cried out to the LORD in their trouble; He saved them out of their distresses. He sent His word and healed them, and delivered them from their destructions. (Psalm 107:19–20)

We know that even as a young man, Jesus knew the Word of God thoroughly. Later, as He entered His ministry and withstood Satan's temptation, He said:

> "It is written, 'Man shall not live on bread alone, but on every word that proceeds out of the mouth of God.'" (Matthew 4:4)

Peter explained that our very spiritual life and health is a result of the Word of God:

> For you have been born again not of seed which is perishable but imperishable, that is, through the living and enduring word of God. (I Peter 1:23)

We could add pages and pages of similar verses that shout the importance of filling our lives with the spiritual nutrition found in Scripture. Let's not ever go hungry!

And let's be sure that our children learn at an early age how to feast on the tasty and complete diet of God's Word.

DEVELOPING GOOD EATING HABITS

Each dad and mom needs to find the best ways to serve the Word in their home. Even after more than twenty years of parenting, we are still discovering fresh approaches to presenting Scripture. Consider implementing some of the following methods of getting more of the Bible into the daily diet of your marriage and family:

- *Read Scripture to each other as a couple.* You don't have to be a theologian or a Bible scholar. Just open the Book and read it. Try a psalm a day. Many men, in particular, get too uptight about being the "spiritual leader in the home." Spiritual leadership is a lifelong process. No one does it perfectly. The easiest thing to do is nothing. Don't be passive; do something! We like to take turns reading the Bible aloud to each other—in our bedroom or even on those rare occasions when we're alone in the car.

- *Memorize Scripture.* Everyone in the family can do this, but children especially are capable of storing away large chunks of the Word of God. A great assortment of Scripture songs and other memory aids are available through Christian bookstores and the Internet.

• *Read the Bible at mealtime.* This is another good way to serve spiritual food. When your children are old enough, let them read, too. There's no need to give sermons or expound on every verse. Just let the Word take root in each heart. If there are comments and questions, take time to listen to and interact with one another.

• *Watch and discuss Christian videos.* Many of the excellent video programs available today—especially those for younger children—will stimulate questions about the Bible and spiritual topics.

• *Enlist your teenager in a Bible study.* I (Dennis) have studied Proverbs with each of our children during their teenage years. We would typically leave the house early before school and talk about a passage over a bagel or doughnut.

This is a great way for a parent to address a specific issue in a teenager's life. During a study with one of our daughters, Rebecca, I showed how Proverbs paints the unflattering picture of a sinful woman who used her sexual powers to trap, seduce, and ultimately destroy a young man. I was able to explain how every woman has a unique, God-given ability through her sexuality to influence a man who is attracted to her. A young woman needs to understand this and not misuse her power, but appropriately conserve it until she is married.

One spring semester I invited another father and his daughter to join us in the study of Proverbs. Not only did the other daughter benefit, but the mutual accountability to do the study weekly was healthy for both of us dads.

• *Display Scripture.* This idea, of course, originates in the challenge issued parents in Deuteronomy to always keep the words of truth everywhere—"on the doorposts of your house and on your gates" (see Deuteronomy 6:6–9).

Write out Scripture passages and hang them throughout the house. I (Barbara) wrote a verse in calligraphy along the tops of the walls in our kitchen. Our children all have the Ten Commandments framed in their rooms.

Tape a special verse for each child on the bathroom mirror. Buy Scripture posters. Play Scripture praise music. Use Scripture screen savers on your computers. The options are many—be creative.

• *Make this a team effort.* Over the years we have seen

the need for both of us to make Scripture a priority in our home. I (Barbara) have read from the Bible to our children in both formal and informal settings. And on occasion I have encouraged Dennis to be more proactive in leading the family in reading Scripture, memorizing verses, and applying the Bible to issues we were facing. Having said that, I know of many single parents who have done a magnificent job of training their children in the Word of God. It can be done (the Lord makes a great team member)!

All of these approaches are effective ways of nurturing your children's spiritual growth. Be wary, however, of relying too much on any one method. Watch for opportunities to teach and apply Scripture in everyday circumstances. Disappointment over a friend who is moving away can be used to teach the principle of giving thanks in all things. Difficulty with a subject at school can move us to pray for wisdom and patience. Sibling rivalry offers a chance to teach what the Bible says about forgiveness. An evening spent gazing at the stars can

SPIRITUAL SEED No. 4

During the routine of the next twenty-four hours, watch for opportunities to present Scripture to your children. See who can come up with the most examples— you or your spouse!

be used to illustrate God's awesome power and love.

When we train our children to know the truth of God's Word, their hearts will be protected from evil.

It may seem at times that children are just not interested in the Bible, but we've found that when they reach high school—where the faith testing really begins—older children start asking questions like "What does the Bible really say about evolution?" or "What does the Bible teach about relating to the opposite sex in an honorable way?"

We've had lively discussions at our dinner table where I (Dennis) sometimes played devil's advocate to help our sons and daughters solidify their beliefs. We directed them to the Bible, and they began to discover truth on their own. That's when their faith roots grew deep.

A critical component in growing a family of faith is your spiritual diet. Seize every opportunity to serve up generous portions of the perfect food—God's Word.

5

SET THE COURSE

The late cartoonist Charles Schultz was a master at injecting life lessons into his "Peanuts" comic strip.

In one installment we see Charlie Brown sitting near the front of a boat. Lucy walks up and says with her usual bite, "Some people go through life with their deck chair facing forward, gazing out where they are going. Others go through life with their deck chair facing backward, looking at where they've been." Lucy then looks directly into Charlie Brown's sunglasses—you know she's ready to let fly with a zinger. "Charlie Brown, which way is your deck chair facing?"

Charlie Brown gives one of his mournful, puzzled looks and answers: "I really don't know—I've never been able to get my deck chair unfolded!"

Sadly, too many families are like poor old Charlie—

adrift at sea about their decisions, values, and activities, unable to get their deck chairs unfolded.

We encourage you, as captain and first mate of your family "boat," to take the time to chart a course that leads to genuine spiritual growth.

LIVE-AND-DIE VALUES

The first step is to define together the we-will-die-for-these values in your family. You both need to agree on these so that you can answer an important question: What do we want to *live* for as a family?

Jesus made several comments that should help you respond:

> "For what will it profit a man if he gains the whole world and forfeits his soul? Or what will a man give in exchange for his soul?" (Matthew 16:26)
>
> "Do not worry then, saying, 'What will we eat?' or 'What will we drink?' or 'What will we wear for clothing?' For the Gentiles eagerly seek all these things; for your heavenly Father knows that you need all these things. But seek first His kingdom and His righteousness, and all these things will be added to you." (Matthew 6:31–33)

It's obvious that we can't just go with the current and

accept the hallowed values of our materialistic culture—career, car, big house in the 'burbs, money, success, and so on. Without much thought, too many Christian families do exactly what their neighbors are doing or what their friends at church are doing. They don't ask themselves, *"Why* are we doing what we're doing?"

TRUE NORTH

Shortly after we started our family, Dennis began to develop a list of everything he wanted to be sure we taught our children. Initially the list had twenty-five values, but that soon ballooned to more than fifty. This was a good exercise, but *fifty*—it was overwhelming! In addition, I (Barbara) was frustrated because Dennis had done this mostly without my involvement. He wasn't purposefully leaving me out; he was just acting on inspiration.

So months later we went away for a weekend and separately wrote down what each of us wanted to build into our children. Next we each prioritized a top-ten values list. Then we came together and worked our way to a unified list of our top-five values. That was a wonderful time of sharing in our relationship, which at the same time established "true north" for our course as parents. From that point on, when issues with our children arose, our list told us whether or not we were on target or drifting.

Many parents, however, have never considered where they are heading with their children. We know that many moms and dads *say* they have a plan for the spiritual development of their children but are not able to clearly explain it. Their plan is not written down.

Baseball star Yogi Berra reportedly once said, "If you don't know where you're going, you'll get there every time." Does that describe you as a parent?

"If you don't know where you're going, you'll get there every time."

SPIRITUAL PRIORITIES

What we are expressing here is not along the lines of "Make sure my child gets into a good college or can find a job after high school"—as important and worthy as those goals may be. We are talking about creating a list of *spiritual* priorities for your children that you will pursue at any cost. Ultimately, you want your children to find the life call and spiritual mission that God wants for them.

A primary spiritual goal for every parent must be to lead each child to a personal relationship with Jesus Christ as Savior and Lord. This requires communicating several basic truths:

- Children need to understand who God is and how He loves them personally:

"For God so loved the world, that He gave
His only begotten Son, that whoever believes
in Him shall not perish, but have eternal life.
For God did not send the Son into the world
to judge the world, but that the world might
be saved through Him." (John 3:16–17)

• Children need to understand that they are
sinners in need of God's forgiveness:

For the wages of sin is death, but the free gift
of God is eternal life in Christ Jesus our Lord.
(Romans 6:23)

• Children need to understand that God's
forgiveness for their sins is received by God's grace
through their faith in Jesus Christ:

For by grace you have been saved through
faith; and that not of yourselves, it is the gift
of God; not as a result of works, so that no one
should boast. (Ephesians 2:8–9)

When we wrote down our family values years ago, we
not only found out who we were and what we valued, but
we also traveled far down the road toward answering a
critical question: How will we measure success? Our
children are not spiritual robots; they must make their own
choices. As parents our responsibility is to bring them up
in the training and instruction of the Lord.

Your spiritual values and goals are bound to differ

somewhat from those of other families. But what's really important is that you and your mate depend prayerfully upon God and hammer out your core family values.

Once the most important values are clarified, then the next step of getting specific about smaller issues comes easier.

Even after agreeing on your family values, it will take effort to keep them in focus. You will need to review these values at least once a year. In addition, changes in values will occur as your family matures, so you need to keep a fresh understanding of where your family needs to be heading.

HANDING OFF THE BATON

Remember that list of twenty-five things we wanted to teach our children? I (Dennis) still carry my dog-eared copy, clearly marked with the top-priority values Barbara and I agreed to. People will sometimes come up after I speak on this topic and ask, "Could I get a copy of your list?" I always say no, because I believe that parents will benefit most from creating their own list.

What's really important is that you and your mate depend prayerfully upon God.

Perhaps it would be helpful, however, if we shared three of the top values on our parenting priority list:

- Teach our children to fear God (Proverbs 1:7).
- Teach our children to love God with all their heart (Matthew 22:37).
- Challenge our children to be involved in accomplishing the great commission (Matthew 28:18–20).

SPIRITUAL SEED NO. 5

Choose a night in the next two weeks when you and your mate can sit down in your deck chairs—or on the living room couch—and create a priority list of values for your children.

(And if you disagree, resist the urge to toss your partner overboard!)

As parents, we need to grasp the reality that we are in what amounts to a spiritual relay race (see Psalm 78:1–8). We have run our lap and now must thrust the baton into our child's hand. The type of handoff we make will determine in part how the next generation follows Jesus Christ. What an honor! What a responsibility! What a privilege!

Let's get those deck chairs unfolded and enjoy the view from a boat headed in the right direction.

6

ROMANCE YOUR MATE

We hate to say this, but sometimes the worst thing that can happen to a couple's romance is for them to get married. *Ouch!*

Why does a book on leading a family spiritually have a chapter on romance? What does romance have to do with raising children in the faith?

Everything. To lead a family spiritually, a husband and wife need to be an intimate team. How much teamwork will there be that really matters if the relationship between mom and dad is boring, strained, cool?

Romance involves the passionate mingling of two souls—a pair of kindred spirit/soul mates who enjoy being with one another. It is true that romance should flow from a relationship where a husband and wife are growing together spiritually. But we also believe that spiritual growth has a better chance in a marriage where each partner enjoys the other. A heart warmed by the love and devotion of a spouse is more open to receiving the love and instruction of Christ.

Although romance certainly should involve music, flowers, and magical evenings, when we say "romance your mate" we're really talking about nurturing your relationship on a day-to-day basis so that the excitement, the fun, the spark, the talk, and the passion do not die. This does not mean that every moment of every day will feel like a raging emotional blaze. But neither will the wood get wet and the campfire die.

We love what Alan Loy McGinnis says in *The Romance Factor:* "Being an artist at romance does not require so much a sentimental or emotional nature as it requires a thoughtful nature. When we think of the romantic things, we think of events that occur because someone made a choice to love. A man...brings his wife a single rose in the evening, a girl makes [the love of her life] a lemon pie with just the degree of tartness he likes.... These are not the goo of sweet emotion, they are the stuff that comes from resolution and determination."[4]

Those are key words—*resolution* and *determination*. Romance is like everything else worth having—there is a sweat-and-perseverance dimension.

We challenge both of you to consider the following ideas for a more romantic marriage.

STUDY YOUR SPOUSE

In the next weeks and months, determine your mate's top three needs—then go all out to satisfy them. Do you know what is discouraging your mate? Do you know what would cause your mate to blossom? Is it an emotional need? Is it a need for conversation? A need for romance?

Or is it a need for something to get done around the house? Is there an issue with forgiveness? Maybe it's something mundane like pulling weeds in the yard, helping put the baby to bed, or cleaning the kitchen after dinner.

One thing we have done over the years is to make a list of those actions that truly please one another. Oftentimes we are so devoted to *our*

SPIRITUAL SEED NO. 6

Write down at least three things that you know will show your love to your soul mate—then make them all happen as soon as possible!

agenda for our mate's life that marriage begins to feel like an institution designed to reform our spouse. Spiritually speaking, you may find that your spouse will have more interest in growing with you in an intimate relationship with God if *you are interested in growing in intimacy with your mate.* By making a list of those things that communicate love, romance, and affection to your spouse you are saying, "I am thinking about you. I like you. I want to be your *sole* soul mate!"

DATE YOUR MATE—GIVE ROMANCE A CHANCE

One of the reasons the fire goes out of a marriage relationship is that we are so busy and preoccupied with the strain of car pools, job pressures, children's needs, and financial challenges. Many are exhausted by the demands of life. Practically speaking, there's little room for cultivating our relationship with one another and thus no chance for romance.

Our children know our relationship is a priority.

One solution is to establish a date night for you as a couple. For nearly fifteen years, Sunday night has been our date night. In fact if we aren't out of the house by 6 P.M., our children start asking if we are going on our date. They *know* our relationship is a priority.

Let us warn you—these dates are sometimes more steak than sizzle! I (Barbara) will never forget one Sunday night rendezvous. One of our teens was stubbornly refusing to cooperate. His attitude had worn me out, and I was in need of perspective. Instead of enjoying each other, we talked nonstop for three hours about how we should deal with this child. Then we prayed. We didn't look into each other's eyes or even look at our calendars. We didn't talk about us. We didn't do anything except focus on this issue. Sometimes our best efforts to spark romance are futile—but we *will* succeed when we stay at it.

Over the years our date night has given us the opportunity to reconnect emotionally, relationally, and spiritually with one another. And after our evening together, we both know how to pray for each other.

GET AWAY FOR THE WEEKEND

Having six children in ten years was one of the biggest challenges to spiritual growth we faced in our first dozen years of marriage. One of the ways we compensated for the emotional drain was to schedule two or three getaways a year. Two nights away from the children will not only give you time to remember why you married one another, but can become a spiritual oasis—a time of renewal and refreshment with one another and God.

Single parents need this kind of break, too. Leave the children with a family member or trusted friend and allow yourself a weekend retreat. Don't feel guilty about it, either—a parent with recharged batteries can more purposefully lead a family.

Some tips for your weekend getaway are in order. Don't turn your time into a packed schedule of events to attend and places to go. Give one another some private moments to read, pray, and spend time alone with God. Pray with and for one another. Pray for your children. Talk with one another about your relationship as a couple and your spiritual relationship with God. Set goals for your spiritual growth as a couple and as a family. Get your calendars out and make them a reflection of your priorities for romance, intimacy, and spiritual growth as a couple.

I (Dennis) have especially fond memories of one of our romantic getaways. After receiving a small windfall of unexpected cash, I was able to plan a trip for the two of us to New England. I made the arrangements—airline, car rental, and baby-sitter. One week before leaving, I sent Barbara on the beginning of a scavenger hunt. She found pieces to a puzzle that, after several hunts, formed a picture of our destination. I swept her away on a leisurely tour of New England filled with walking, talking, and taking pictures. It reminded us of the slow pace of our honeymoon.

Out of such pleasurable experiences emerges a new resolve to work together to see a family become all God desires for it. And it makes marriage a whole lot more fun!

Here are a few more ideas on getting the sizzle back in your romance.

• Court your wife. If you question the need for this, see what God reveals in the Song of Solomon. Solomon and his bride knew how to stir the passions of their love for each other through creative courting.

• Write your husband an old-fashioned love letter. Don't make it the kind of letter you would like to receive, but the kind he would like to receive.

Don't let your marriage get in the way of your romance!

• Bring your wife a rose. Hand her the flower, take her in your arms, touch her face gently, look into her eyes, and say, "I want you to know that marrying you was the smartest thing I ever did, sweetheart. I would do it all over again." (Warning: Some men may need to have an oxygen tank handy for resuscitation purposes at this point!)

Don't let your marriage get in the way of your romance! The warmer your relationship, the better you will function as a team in leading your family spiritually.

7

TRAIN YOUR DISCIPLES

Parents fulfill many important roles for their children: cook, innkeeper, medic, taxi driver, coach…the list is long. But there's one role that is often overlooked or misunderstood—disciple maker.

Do you see yourself as a trainer of disciples? If not, here's why you should: You have been called to "make disciples of all the nations" (Matthew 28:19). And in making disciples, your family is your number one responsibility. Fathers, in fact, are specifically directed to "bring [your children] up in the discipline and instruction of the Lord" (Ephesians 6:4).

Children learn everything important about life from their parents. Does that sober you like it sobers us? From his first moments, your little tyke has a marvelous "antenna farm" of senses that never stop picking up data from the big people roaming through his life. Things like: *How do people talk to one another? How is love expressed? How do people get attention? Who does what around this place? Am I important?*

Whether we like it or not, our words and actions are observed, evaluated, and stored by these remarkable little people God places in our care. This must be one reason that the Bible teaches how we are to instruct our children about faith:

> "And these words, which I am commanding you today, shall be on your hearts. You shall teach them diligently to your sons and shall talk of them when you sit in your house and when you walk by the way and when you lie down and when you rise up.... You shall write them on the door-posts of your house and on your gates." (Deuteronomy 6:6–9)

So when it comes to building spiritual strength in our children, guess who the main contractors are? Good ol' dad and mom! Certainly children will acquire spiritual knowledge from other sources—church and Sunday school, for example. But we parents are the ones who make the biggest impact because our disciples hang out with us more than anyone else.

PLUGGING INTO GOD

I (Dennis) remember a morning our ten-year-old daughter Ashley didn't want me to fly on an airplane. As I began to back the car out of the garage, Ashley came running out to give me a hug. I could tell something was troubling her. Reaching through the car window to hold her hand, I asked, "What's wrong, Princess?"

"I'm afraid your airplane is going to crash," she said. A recent airplane accident in Dallas had scared her.

"Planes are even safer than cars, Ashley," I said, trying to reassure her. "Besides, my life is in God's hands, and He knows what He's doing." By this time Ashley was holding my large hand with both of her small ones. Fear was in her face.

"Ashley, being afraid is normal for all of us. But you can give it to God," I said. "You're in the process of learning how to depend less on me and more on Him." She still looked unconvinced and grasped my hand tighter than ever. "I won't always be here to answer your questions—but God will."

At this moment I received some inspiration on how to help Ashley understand. "It's as if there are invisible electrical cords coming from you to me and your mom," I said. "As you grow up, it's our responsibility to unplug those electrical wires from us and teach you how to plug them into God."

I took one of her hands and gently "unplugged" one invisible cord. Ashley frowned, then grinned as I guided her hand above her head and helped her visualize plugging into God.

"Ashley," I said, "I need to go, and you're going to have to take your fear to Jesus Christ. He can give you peace."

As parents, our assignment is to plug our children into God. Our model in this process is the greatest teacher in history—the Lord Jesus. In a way, the disciples were His family. He poured His life into them. He asked them to follow Him around so that they could see Him live His life. And along the way He taught them what they needed to know, often using vivid, memorable object lessons based on what they were experiencing together. We can learn a lot about discipleship training from His example.

As parents, our assignment is to plug our children into God.

BASIC TRAINING

Here are four ideas on basic discipleship training:

Effective training requires seeing the goal clearly. Many moms and dads have no clear idea of what they want to build into their children spiritually. Beyond salvation, what kind of relationship with God are you seeking for your children? What do you expect them to know about God's Word and the Christian life? What values and character qualities are you praying for?

We've already mentioned how important it is to have a list of the spiritual lessons you want to teach your children. It will become a foundation that you'll turn to again and again. But don't stop there: Train your children to walk with God and obey Him.

Effective training involves a plan and strategy. How do you expect to accomplish your spiritual goals for each child? You don't need too many details, but have key objectives written down and review them every year.

Effective training requires repetition. A Green Beret once told us, "As Green Berets, we train to learn what to do in every conceivable circumstance—over and over and over again. Then in times of battle we know what to do. It's just second nature to us." Don't expect a child to get it on the first try—or even the fiftieth. This is a draining aspect of parenting. But you simply must press on—continuing to exhort and encourage your child in the disciplines of staying in the center of God's will.

Effective training must include standards and accountability. Disciple is the root word for *discipline.* Thus, disciple making includes consistent and appropriate discipline.

There is an old saying: You cannot expect that which

you do not inspect. Throughout a child's growing-up years, parents will continue to work on the basics—obedience, self-control, honesty, kindness to others, unselfishness, and so on. This is obviously a critical component in building spiritual strength. A frequent mistake made by parents is to give children too much freedom without appropriate oversight. This is especially true in a family of more than one child. Parents tend to over-control their first child and then relax too much with the second and other younger children.

PRACTICAL DISCIPLE MAKING

You may be thinking, *Those are great concepts, but how can I apply them so that disciple making at home actually works?* Here are some practical tips:

- Have daily devotions and/or weekly family nights. This is an old idea that never goes out of style—and never stops being a challenge. Most Christian families struggle to do this consistently and well (we know this firsthand!). The key is to set aside your feelings of inadequacy and any memories of past disasters and *stick with it.*

    Many excellent resources are available for family nights, including the Heritage Builders series published by Focus on the Family. Our favorite daily devotional in recent years has been *On This*

Day—a series of stories about courageous acts of faith throughout history.

• Go on a short-term mission trip with your older children. We know of no better way to teach them how to look at the world through the eyes of Jesus Christ and refine their values. A number of years ago we took three of our children to China and had a wonderful time sharing Christ with nationals and interacting with career missionaries. We even smuggled Bibles into the country.

But don't feel you have to travel far to model the love of Jesus. Volunteer to serve a meal in a downtown church soup kitchen. Or offer to clean up the yard of an elderly woman in your neighborhood. You can create a meaningful missionary experience for your sons and daughters in another country or in your own hometown.

• Attend family camps and conferences. Over the years we've used special spiritual events to "grow" our family. These times not only exposed our children to a concentrated time in God's Word but also provided opportunities for them to meet other great followers of Christ. Some of the finest conferences for teenagers are hosted by Student Venture, a ministry of Campus Crusade for Christ. Held in the summer months and over Christmas vacation, these conferences will challenge your teen to become a true follower of Christ. (For information, check out www.studentventure.org on the Internet or call 800-699-4678.)

Whatever methods you choose, we encourage you to embrace what may be the most important role you play as a parent—*disciple maker.* No one else will have a better opportunity to make a great follower of Jesus than you.

Chuck Swindoll summarizes this eloquently:

> Whatever else may be said about the home, it is the bottom line of life, the anvil upon which attitudes and convictions are hammered out. It is the place where life's bills come due, [it is] the single most influential force in our earthly existence.... It is at home, among family members, that we come to terms with circumstances. It is here life makes up its mind.[5]

SPIRITUAL SEED No. 7

Sit down with your spouse and review the tips listed here. Which would work in your family? Which would be the most productive? Choose one of these, or an idea of your own, and give it a try this week!

8

FIGHT THE DARKNESS

Have you ever had a day where it felt that from morning until night you and your family were in vicious spiritual battle against the unseen "bad guys"?

Anyone building a family of spiritual vitality must develop offensive and defensive tactics against our enemy. Scripture makes it clear: "Put on the full armor of God, so that you will be able to stand firm against the schemes of the devil. For our struggle is not against flesh and blood, but against the rulers, against the powers, against the world forces of this darkness, against the spiritual forces of wickedness in the heavenly places" (Ephesians 6:11–12).

The battle lines form in every Christian home over what often appear to be innocent matters. To show you what we mean, let's spend a morning with a fictional family we'll call the Smiths. The parents, George and Marsha, are veteran combat warriors against evil. They've been married twenty years, are in their forties, and have two children—Tonya (age sixteen) and Luke (age thirteen).

George's alarm rings—it's seven-thirty on Saturday morning. He sighs and rolls out of bed, giving Marsha a kiss as he exits. George would like another hour of sleep, but he knows after years of battling against evil on behalf of his family that if he doesn't stay spiritually fit, he won't have the edge he needs.

George spends thirty minutes reading and meditating on God's Word, praying, and praising the King.

George stumbles past piles of dirty laundry into the kitchen, where he downs a breakfast of coffee and toast. Then he shuts the door to a spare room in the basement and spends thirty minutes reading and meditating on God's Word, praying, and praising the King. George also notes in his prayer journal the important spiritual issues likely to face his family in the next twenty-four hours.

When George surfaces from the basement, Marsha is finishing her bowl of granola. "Do you want a few minutes to yourself?" he asks. "I'll take kitchen patrol."

Marsha smiles and nods her agreement, then heads to the bedroom to do her own spiritual preparation.

Luke bursts into the kitchen, nearly knocking Marsha over. "Sorry, Mom," he says. He grabs a cereal bowl from the cupboard. "Hi, Dad. Hey, I've got a soccer game at ten—you coming?"

"I don't think I can this morning—but Mom will go. I'll come to your Wednesday game."

"Okay. And Dad?" Luke pours a bowlful of Frosted Flakes as he talks. "Rob wants me to come over after the game and hang out and spend the night. Can I go?"

"Sounds like fun. Have you done your Saturday chores?"

"Oh yeah, I can get that stuff done before the game. So can I go to Rob's?"

"Well, tell me a little more. What are you doing this afternoon?"

"Rob said maybe his mom would take us to the mall and we could see a movie."

"Which movie do you think you'll go to?"

"Ah, Rob and I were thinking about *Destiny Death*—it's a great action movie with Kasper Kong in it."

George remembers seeing a violent advertisement for *Destiny Death* on TV. "Is that really a movie you should see? What's it rated?"

"Not sure, Dad."

"Tell you what, Luke," George says. "I'm going to check out that movie on the Internet." George logs onto the family computer and finds a Web site that describes movie plots and lists objectionable material. As he suspected, *Destiny Death* is rated PG-13 and includes much violence, a sexual encounter between Kasper Kong's character and a woman police officer, and extensive use of obscene language. He notices that the name of Jesus Christ is used as a curse word five times.

"Oh, boy," George mutters to himself as he walks back to the kitchen. "Hey, Luke, I'm not sure that's a good movie to see."

"Dad!" Luke grimaces. "I never get to see the good adventure flicks. Everybody at school watches them. What's the big deal?"

"I'm going to check out that movie on the Internet."

"You know we have rules about what you watch, Luke," George says. "Look, I'll call Rob's mom and we'll talk it through."

"No, Dad! That's embarrassing—" Luke stops when he sees the look on George's face. "Oh, whatever!" He takes his dishes to the kitchen sink and marches out of the room.

George stares at the phone on the wall. *Let me have a root canal instead of this!* he thinks. Then he remembers promising the Lord only thirty minutes ago that he would be the protector of his family today. "Okay, stud, make the call," he mutters. He phones Rob's mom and introduces himself.

"Hey, thanks for letting Rob invite Luke over," he says. "Luke tells me they might see this movie *Destiny Death* today, and I was wondering—"

"Oh, we haven't decided on which movie yet. Is that a good one?"

> George stares at the phone on the wall. Let me have a root canal instead of this!

"Actually, I checked the Internet and found out it's got a lot of fighting and bad language."

"Really. Well, we'll have to find something else."

"I'm glad to hear you agree with me. If you want, I'll do some more checking on other new movies. Maybe there's something better."

"Please do. Could we talk about it at the soccer game?"

"Sure, I'll tell Marsha what I find out, and she can give you the details."

George hangs up, relieved that there was no conflict with Rob's mom. He checks his watch: nine-thirty. He feels like taking a nap. Instead, he searches for Luke and finds him in his bedroom.

"Hey, Luke, I talked to Rob's mom," George says. "She doesn't want Rob to watch *Destiny Death* either."

Looking disappointed, Luke plops down on his bed. "Dad," he says, his head down, "most of the guys have seen it already. They say it's not that bad."

"I know it's disappointing to feel like you're missing something," George says. "But Mom and I need to say no when we think it's important. And this is a time I think it's important."

Luke looks out the window, so George continues. "It's not that we like making you unhappy, Luke. We make these decisions because we love you. Do you know that?"

This time Luke glances up. "Yeah, I know." After a few seconds he speaks again. "So can Rob and I still see a movie?"

"You bet. Why don't you get ready for the game, then we'll look on the computer and pick something together."

Luke stands up. "Okay. Thanks, Dad."

George tousles his son's hair. Luke almost smiles.

Returning to the kitchen, George finds Marsha with an arm around their daughter, Tonya, who is sobbing at the table.

"What's going on?" George asks. Tonya raises her tearstained face but doesn't reply. Marsha gives her husband one of those it-would-be-better-if-you-left-us-alone looks. George knows Tonya is struggling with a boyfriend who is insanely immature. George wonders what new crisis has emerged. He motions to Marsha and they step into the hallway. "What happened?"

"Johnny really came on physically to Tonya last night."

"Don't you think it's about time for Johnny to hit the road?" George says, a wave of hot, red color climbing his neck.

"Well, let us talk it through, okay? Do you mind driving Luke to his game?"

George sees his Saturday plans disintegrating. "No, I guess not. But I don't know how I'm going to get the garage cleaned today."

"First things first, honey," Marsha says before returning to Tonya.

"Hey, Luke! Get your stuff—I'm taking you to the game," George calls, grabbing his baseball hat and keys and heading for the garage door. Then he remembers. "But meet me at the computer first." Quickly he logs onto the Internet. They need to have a movie to recommend when they see Rob's mom.

THIS IS SPIRITUAL WARFARE?

Does George and Marsha's story resonate with you? If it doesn't, it will. While raising six teenagers, we have encountered situations like this on a daily basis. The enemy of our souls wants to destroy our families one inch, one decision at a time. As parents, it is our job to recognize the threat and do battle against the evil that lurks without and within. Sometimes we fight well and sometimes we don't. But if we are to grow our family spiritually, battle we must.

Here are some types of evil that threaten our home—and yours, too:

- *Rotten ideas from the culture*—For example, what society feeds us in regard to relationships, divorce, abortion, sex outside of marriage, materialism, and more.
- *Media pollution*—Many TV shows are raunchy, and the advertising is often appalling; movies increasingly push to the edge; music can be gross or incredibly suggestive.
- *The Internet*—Pornographic filth is just one click away.
- *Teenage retail stores that market more than just clothing*—Businesses like Abercrombie & Fitch promote sexually suggestive and explicit posters and catalogs.
- *Hyper-materialism*—Constant pressure to have more and more.
- *Physical dangers*—Date rape, drugs, random violence at school, incredible pressure related to appearance and weight (especially for teenage girls).
- *Other "Christian" families*—Their values look the

same as yours, but in reality are not substantially different from the values of the world.

• *Evil in our hearts*—All of us battle against the pull of the flesh. As Jesus said, "For out of the heart come evil thoughts, murders, adulteries, fornications, thefts, false witness, slanders. These are the things which defile the man" (Matthew 15:19–20).

Our enemy is a clever deceiver. Without question this list is too small. Be on guard and ready to do battle on behalf of your family.

BATTLE PREPARATION

As parents, we are called to take on our spiritual enemies on behalf of our children. If you and your family are to grow spiritually, you must know how to protect your family and go on the offensive. Here are some suggestions:

• Realize that you and your family live on a spiritual battlefield. God's reputation and eternity are at stake in the decisions you and your children make.

• Realize that your mate is not your enemy. Go to war beside your mate against your common enemy!

• Stand firm and let God's Word be your guide. Put on your full armor. We are on the winning side—let's act like it! (See Ephesians 6:13–17.)

• Pray without ceasing, and give thanks in everything. (See I Thessalonians 5:17–18.) Prayer is one of your more important resources in the battle for your family.

• Don't take temptation lightly; flee immorality. (See 2 Timothy 2:22.) Guard your heart! (See Proverbs 4:23.)

• Walk by faith, not by what you feel and see. Since God and His Word are completely trustworthy, our faith is the difference. Sink your teeth into God's Word and don't let go. (See 2 Corinthians 5:7.)

•Join forces with others fighting evil. Don't be passive; go on the offensive. The body of Christ is mighty when we unite and employ our gifts and other resources.

Fighting the darkness with offensive and defensive weapons is critical if we are to have spiritually strong families. Let's gear up and head to the battlefront—which for most of us is as close as the kitchen.

SPIRITUAL SEED No. 8

If your children are old enough, talk with them about the evil that surrounds us—and about how they can face evil with confidence by putting on the "armor of God." Begin by teaching them to pray.

9

REST AND REFRESH

Is Sunday any different from the other days of the week for you and your family? If not, you are missing out on not only physical refreshment but spiritual restoration as well. One of the most profound and powerful principles in all of Scripture is that spiritual rest precedes spiritual growth. That's what the Sabbath is all about.

God knows that after six days of work and effort, everyone needs a break. That's why He commanded, "You shall work six days, but on the seventh day you shall rest; even during plowing time and harvest you shall rest" (Exodus 34:21). That's the reason for the Sabbath—to give us regularly scheduled time to relax, reflect, think critically about life, and find a time of peace where we can clearly hear the voice of our Father. This is when parents can regroup and refocus on what needs to happen spiritually in their own lives and within their family in the coming week.

We know that in our culture many people have to work on Sunday—including, of course, pastors and church staff who help us worship. But what counts is the *idea* of the Sabbath. Some people will have to observe their rest and refreshment on a day other than Sunday.

I (Barbara) have long felt strongly that Sunday be a day set apart for this purpose. I've always been particularly impressed by the second half of the passage mentioned above: "Even during plowing time and harvest you shall rest." In other words, no matter how busy the family is or how many items remain on the to-do list, we must have a period of calm one day each week.

We don't want our children so busy that they can't hear God's still voice.

Adjusting to a Sabbath pace can be stressful; until you get used to it, slowing down to rest takes work! This is not easy, especially for a large family like ours. But we want our children to understand that something about Sunday should be different. We don't want them to grow up and be so frantically stimulated and busy that they can't hear God's still voice.

Despite our determination, we still have a long way to go in really capturing what God has in mind for the

Sabbath. We do try to make Sunday different from other days. We'll take a nap, or read a book, or play a game that's fun but not too demanding; yard work is normally off-limits. And usually Dennis and I have our weekly date on Sunday evening—a meal and time to talk, plan, and realign our lives with what we believe God wants for our family.

Here are some tips for creating your own quality Sabbath experience:

• A good Sabbath starts at least the day before. For example, if any homework is due at school on Monday, we ask our children to complete it by Saturday night. On Sunday we go to church. For the remainder of the day, phone use is limited. That keeps the house quieter—an atmosphere conducive to naps, reading, relationship building, and light recreation. Anxiety builders like paying bills or trying to balance the checkbook are generally avoided.

• Worship is key. Be sure to attend church and continue to worship in your heart at home after the service. Fill the house with hymns and praise music that exalts our great God.

• Enjoy time together as a family. Spending a few hours in God's creation (hiking, fishing, playing at a park) after church can be a wonderful way of refreshing the soul and of reestablishing relationships in a busy family.

• Don't get uptight. Observing the Sabbath should not turn into a legalistic burden. It's the principle that counts. In our busy culture, you will have Sundays that are anything but restful. But stick with it. Keep refining how to make this special day fun and restful.

SPIRITUAL SEED No. 9

Discuss with your mate how you can make this Sunday—or another day in the next week— a time of rest. Then, at the end of your Sabbath, compare notes on how refreshed you feel!

We were reminded again of the importance of the Sabbath after the unforgettable events of September 11, 2001. From Tuesday morning until Saturday evening our TV screens were filled with heart-breaking images of the attacks on the Pentagon and World Trade Center towers. Our family needed Sunday, September 16—a day set aside to worship God and pray—to regain perspective. It was indeed a needed Sabbath rest for all of us.

If we followers of Jesus seek more rest on Sundays, we will reap clearer minds, more relaxed spirits, and peace-filled hearts in our home. The result will be deeper spiritual roots and greater fruitfulness for Christ and His Kingdom.

10

KEEP YOUR COVENANT

Will you be committed to Barbara if she someday commits adultery?"

You can imagine how I (Dennis) winced when the friend who was giving us premarital counseling asked that question. And then before I could answer, he turned and asked Barbara the same thing: "Will you remain committed to Dennis if he someday becomes an adulterer?"

What the man wanted to do was shock us with the sobering reality of what it means to enter into a covenant—not just with the man or woman you will marry but also with God Himself. The keeping of a covenant is very important to almighty God. He keeps His word. He's a covenant keeper. So if we want to please Him and in the process create the relational environment where a marriage and family can flourish spiritually, we need to take the marriage covenant very seriously.

If you are thinking, *Well, I have no intention of ever divorcing my spouse and breaking up our family—I can skip this chapter,* let us make clear that covenant breaking does not include just adultery or divorce. Many a husband and wife have betrayed their marriage covenant by attitudes and actions directed toward a spouse.

When you pledged your vows and entered into a covenant with God and your spouse, you promised more than not to get a divorce. Your marriage covenant was a guarantee that you would love, cherish, honor, care for, sacrifice for, and give up your life on behalf of your mate. If spiritual growth and vitality are to be experienced in your family the way God intended, then the sacred vows that we made to one another need to be fulfilled.

We are especially concerned about two threats to the marriage covenant that are particularly destructive today.

THE D WORD

To make your marriage all it can be, avoid the word *divorce.* Never let the *D* word come out of your lips. Vow before God that from this day forward you will never say this word in any kind of conversation with your spouse.

Research indicates that once the *D* word is uttered, it becomes a very real possibility for both speaker and hearer.

Threatening your spouse with the *D* word and in the hearing of children is like hooking them up to an intravenous solution of fear. Instead, use the *C* words: *covenant* and *commitment.*

Now if you have blown it and the *D* word has escaped your lips, may we encourage you to repent? Ask God to forgive you. Gather your spouse and children and ask them to forgive you for threatening a divorce or for considering it as an option. Then change your ways and excise the *D* word from your vocabulary.

At FamilyLife we received a letter that explains a child's perspective on divorce. This young woman in her twenties wrote to me (Dennis):

> *Threatening your family with the D word is like hooking them up to an intravenous solution of fear.*

I just listened to your broadcast...and felt compelled to write. You mentioned that you received a letter from someone concerned that you are "too hard" on divorce, and my heart broke.

I am a twenty-eight-year-old single professional woman. I grew up in an unstable, non-Christian home. I have (to date) had five parents and three sets of siblings. My mother called me just this past Sunday to inform me that she is about to bestow upon me a sixth parent and fourth set of siblings. I understand in the very depths of my being why my God hates divorce and why we should, too. No good thing comes from it. Ever. Divorce has stolen from me not only a family, but also a trust that marriage is a good and desirable thing. The grapes my parents ate with relish have set my teeth on edge. Divorce answers no question, solves no problem, resolves no conflict, gives no respite, restores no dignity, and grants no peace.

Divorce cannot be dealt with too harshly, especially in the church of Jesus Christ. I bless God that He knows no divorce in this marriage covenant He has established between Himself and His bride! Thank you for your commitment to teach husbands and wives to honor the covenant they made before God, if for no other reason than the sake of the next generation.[6]

Do you understand why we never want to use the *D* word or do anything else that threatens our marriage covenant?

THE SECRET SIN

This one applies most often to men but affects increasing

numbers of women: pornography. It is a problem for millions of Christians today. No marriage bed has room for three people, but that's the situation when one partner brings in fantasies based on pornographic images.

Pornography is an affront to God's idea of holy marriage. It is an adulterous affair of the heart. It is deceitful. The person viewing pornography is giving his heart and dreams to someone other than his wife. A deliberate choice to look at pornography is an act of betrayal of the marriage covenant.

If you are involved with pornography at any level, you must break free by repenting.

Pornography once was largely confined to certain parts of town or certain kinds of magazines. But now it's instantly available in your home via the Internet.

If you are involved with pornography at any level, you must break free by repenting. Call out to the Lord Jesus for His help to break free. You will find grace, forgiveness, and power. And it is *very* important that you seek out an accountability partner who will stand beside you in the battle. Seek counseling if necessary. Most importantly, come clean with your spouse (a godly counselor will be needed at this point in most marriages).

We believe that pornography is one of the leading causes of marital destruction today. Don't allow a secret sin to create dry rot in your life, your marriage, and your family. Why would you want to allow something like this to become the gateway for evil to enter your home? God won't allow you to persist in such sin without calling you to account. He will settle up with you. He sees and knows, but He also offers all the grace and forgiveness that you need. We encourage and admonish you to reveal your struggle to your spouse so that spiritual growth and fruitfulness may be in your home in abundance.

THE COST AND THE GLORY

Several years ago, Barbara and I learned at a deeper level what our marriage covenant might require in the future.

I was at the office when I noticed a magazine story about Robertson and Muriel McQuilkin. Dr. McQuilkin was president of Columbia Bible College and Seminary (now Columbia International University) for twenty-two years. As is often true in such cases, during all those years Muriel backed up Robertson on the home front and served him in many other ways as the president's wife. They were an effective ministry team.

Sadly, Muriel's health deteriorated; tests confirmed that she had Alzheimer's disease. In time her abilities failed, and Robertson became increasingly responsible for her basic needs, which included feeding, bathing, and dressing. Muriel's reasoning skills were lost and she slurred her words.

With Muriel's needs escalating and his responsibilities at the college unchanged, Robertson faced a torturous decision: Should he place Muriel in an institution? He wanted to honor God's call on his life as a college and seminary president, but he also had made a covenant to stand by his wife no matter what life brought. In the article, Dr. McQuilkin wrote,

> When the time came, the decision was firm. It took no great calculation. It was a matter of integrity. Had I not promised, 42 years before, "in sickness and in health...till death do us part"?[7]

I was so moved by the story of the McQuilkins that I called Barbara at home and read portions to her. When I told her that Robertson had chosen to resign as president of the college and seminary so he could care for his Muriel, Barbara began to cry.

"What's wrong, sweetheart?" I asked.

After a lengthy silence, Barbara answered, her voice breaking, "Dennis, will you love me like that?"

"Yes, I will," I answered softly but without reservation.

I agreed totally with what Robertson McQuilkin wrote in explaining why he had quit his job and gone home to care for Muriel:

This was no grim duty to which I was stoically resigned, however. It was only fair. She had, after all, cared for me for almost four decades with marvelous devotion; now it was my turn. And such a partner she was! If I took care of her for 40 years, I would never be out of her debt.[8]

All of us owe a debt like that to the one we pledged our life to at the altar. But as Robertson said, this is not "grim duty." Rather, it is a glorious opportunity to walk in the footsteps of Jesus in caring for one of His precious lambs. Most of us will never have to go through a trial like that of the McQuilkins. But doesn't it fill you with confidence and security to know that there is someone who loves you so much that you would never face such an ordeal alone?

By keeping your marriage covenant holy, you will honor God, build a tower of relational strength and stability, and bring quiet joy and security to every member of your family.

SPIRITUAL SEED No. 10

Tonight, hold hands, look each other in the eye, and remind each other how committed you are to building a holy and secure marriage and family—no matter what.

ENJOY THE JOY!

If you are feeling even a little overwhelmed by the challenges of growing a spiritually strong family, we have an encouraging word for you: *Enjoy!*

Does that surprise you, the notion that leading your small band of pilgrims through enemy territory should be a joyful—even *fun*—experience?

Too many Christian parents are known by their permanent grimaces. Lighten up! Lift your eyes from the mucky plain of daily life to the horizon of promise! God desires what you desire: the salvation and abundant life of your—and His—precious offspring. He delights in you and them. He longs to shower His richest benefits on your little band. This is cause for celebration—for many laughs and triumphant good spirits on the parenting road.

God designed the family to be a spiritual garden that

grows flowers for today and seeds for tomorrow. It is the single most important place where faith is planted and hope is nurtured. This garden must endure weeds from previous generations, present-day droughts, and future attacks. Yet when all else in the culture perishes, the family committed to Jesus Christ stands strong and enjoys sweet rewards, both now and for generations to come.

Our day-to-day purpose and level of involvement change as our sons and daughters mature and eventually leave the nest. But we should not buy into the world's view that our impact diminishes as we age. The psalmist wrote, "The righteous...will flourish...in the courts of our God. They will still yield fruit in old age; they shall be full of sap and very green" (Psalm 92:12–15).

God wants you to flourish, to be sap-filled and green when you are old! Grow today so that you'll enjoy a green tomorrow. Cling to this truth as the years pass: You play a vital role as mentor and spiritual leader of your family. We parents have the awesome, joyful privilege of sowing godly seed—not just in the generation of our children but also in the generation of our children's children.

Barbara and I have already tasted a few bites of the delicious fruit awaiting. I remember well the day we brought our oldest son, Benjamin, to a large state university. He and I walked outside the student housing complex for some fresh air and sat on the tailgate of a truck. A stream of young men passed by, most of them drinking.

I became fearful for my son. I wanted to take my "arrow" and put it back in the quiver, to not aim and release it into this "crooked and perverse generation." I looked Benjamin in the eye and said, "Son, I've got to tell you that watching all these young men get wasted on booze really makes me question the wisdom of sending you into the middle of all this."

After a pause, Benjamin lifted his eyes to mine. "Dad, this is my mission field. It's going to be tough, but if it were easy these guys wouldn't need Jesus Christ. This is what you and Mom have trained me for. God has led me here and He will protect me."

My eyes surrendered tears; indescribable joy welled up from my heart. *Yes!* Obeying God in raising the next generation to carry out His purposes on the earth is worth the daily sacrifices.

Dear Mom and Dad—hang in there! If you persevere in applying the godly principles in this book, you too will experience such joyful moments. Do as the apostle Paul urged: "Press on toward the goal for the prize of the upward call of God in Christ Jesus" (Philippians 3:14).

Lead your family to a steadfast commitment to God and His purposes. Your family garden will grow spiritually abundant fruit when you persist in doing well!

And remember to enjoy the joy of the journey.

ENDNOTES

1. FamilyLife, "Top 10 Most Common Needs," Family Needs Survey, National Database (FamilyLife, Little Rock, Arkansas, 2001).

2. Barna Research Online, "Annual Study Reveals America Is Spiritually Stagnant," 5 March 2001. http://www.barna.org/cgi-bin/PagePressRelease.asp?PressReleaseID=84&Reference=B (accessed 8 October 2001).

3. FamilyLife, "Spiritual Activity—Related to Reading/Discussing the Bible," Family Needs Survey, National Database (FamilyLife, Little Rock, Arkansas, 2001).

4. Alan Loy McGinnis, *The Romance Factor* (New York: Harper & Row, 1982), 198.

5. Charles Swindoll, *Home Is Where Life Makes Up Its Mind* (Portland, Ore.: Multnomah, 1979), 5.

6. Private correspondence. Used by permission.

7. Robertson McQuilkin, "Living by Vows," *Christianity Today,* 8 October 1990, 40.

8. Ibid., 40.

The publisher and author would love
to hear your comments about this book.

PLEASE CONTACT US AT:
www.familyfirstseries.com

EFFECTIVELY DEVELOPING GODLY FAMILIES

• • • • • • • •

FamilyLife has focused on building marriages and homes since 1976. Today we are equipping millions in the United States and overseas. Here are some creative and effective ways that FamilyLife can strengthen your home:

- ◆ Connect at **conferences** such as our "Weekend to Remember," I Still Do™ one-day event for couples, and church-sponsored seminars.

- ◆ Use studies from the **HomeBuilders Couples Series®** to learn God's plan for marriage in an encouraging small-group setting.

- ◆ Tune in to our **broadcasts** for practical, biblical marriage and parenting information—"FamilyLife Today," "FamilyLife This Week," "Living a Legacy," "Real FamilyLife with Dennis Rainey," and "Revive Our Hearts."

- ◆ Discover a growing line of **resources** designed to equip you and give you tools to build and strengthen your family.

- ◆ Access **www.familylife.com** twenty-four hours a day for a wide range of helpful tools for your marriage and family.

FAMILYLIFE™
Bringing Timeless Principles Home

Dennis Rainey, Executive Director
P.O. Box 8220 ◆ Little Rock, Arkansas 72221-8220
1-800-FL-TODAY ◆ www.familylife.com
A division of Campus Crusade for Christ